IONA and S via OBAN

Nostalgic Album Views

Bob Charnley

Published by

CLAN BOOKS
The Cross, Doune
Perthshire FK16 6BE
Tel: 0786 841330
Fax: 0786 841326

First published 1994

ISBN 1 873597 02 9

Typeset in NewCenturySchoolbook
Adlard Print & Typesetting Services
The Old School
The Green
Ruddington
Notts NG11 6HH

CONTENTS:

"I am no melancholy mourner of the past, rather a sanguine believer in progress and the future; but alas! whenever I look on the lonely ruins among the hills, I feel inclined to sing a Dirge."

(Robert Buchanan - **'The Hebrid Isles'** - 1883 edition)

Dedication

Quite simply – for Sandra.

In 1969 we landed on Iona from *King George V*. It was a *first* for both of us but it was also our honeymoon!

This book, therefore, is a surprise Silver Wedding present, somewhat like the surprise she had twenty-five years ago when she was bodily gathered-up by a burly sailor aboard *King George V* and deposited in a small boat for the trip across to the island!

OBAN, FROM S-W. 2176 G.W.W.

OBAN – GATEWAY TO THE ISLES OF YOUTH!

IN Victorian times, the more adventurous tourist sailed off to St. Kilda to spot puffin and *gawp* at the natives on their remote wind-swept isle. Edwardian gentlemen, on the other hand, journeyed to North and South Uist to fish for trout. Yet even they were tempted to spend a part of their day peering at the natives in their isolated hamlets, for these dusky strange-tongued islanders living in rude stone huts were – to the natives of Glasgow, Manchester or London – some of the very strangest of all the inhabitants in a great Great Britain.

But Iona was different; Iona provided no such culture shock. To this small island the tourist came to view the historic remains; to gaze upon the ancient crosses and the Royal tombs; to stare at the long-abandoned nunnery and the derelict cathedral but *not* at the islanders. And at the end of an exciting day, the visitors returned to the warmth and comfort of their Oban hotels, tired and ravenous, perhaps a little sea-sick, but spiritually satisfied for they had made the ultimate pilgrimage to Iona and seen the wonders of Fingal's Cave.

MᶜLEAN'S CROSS.   Sᵀ MARTIN'S CROSS.

Victorian lithograph of Iona c.1880.

Somewhat less than modest in his description of these two islands at the end of the last century, a local guide-book writer claimed that they were "... *among the shrines of Europe*", and from most of Europe they came – the French, the Germans, the Italians and all those other *"Continental strangers"*. By the boat-load they crossed to Iona, intent on following in the footsteps of the saintly, the good and the famous – or simply strolling in the wake of a few who had none of these worthy attributes – for Iona, being less remote than St. Kilda or South Uist, was ideal for the casual day-tripper. Here, the natives were regarded as *normal* people living in *quaint* rather than rude homes, although when Doctor Samuel Johnson visited the place with James Boswell in 1773 he felt it necessary to comment that the people appeared *"...remarkably gross and remarkably neglected"*.

Doubtless overcome by their arrival on a moonlit October night – the very end of the tourist season now as the hoteliers prepare to close their doors until Easter – Boswell reacted somewhat emotionally and *"cordially embraced"* Johnson, describing him in his **'Journal of a Tour to the Hebrides'** as a *"great and pious friend"*. This showy piece of affection, however, may have had more to do with Boswell's relief at being on dry land rather than a constant urge to hug his companion. In the absence of a suitable landing-place the intrepid duo had been carried ashore by the boatmen – *"Our Highlanders"* as Johnson called them – and this noble gesture was all the more generous when one reads Boswell's contemporary description of the good doctor: *"large, robust ... approaching to the gigantick, and grown unwieldy from corpulency."*

Dr. Samuel Johnson (1709-1784)

In August 1847, seventy-four years after Johnson and Boswell had been lifted from their little boat, a somewhat grander yacht arrived off Iona during a cruise from Crinan to Staffa.

This time the islanders were prepared, looking neither gross nor neglected. The street had been swept. The constables were at their designated points. The landing-place was secured. But Her Majesty Queen Victoria declined to leave the royal yacht! It was Albert of Saxe-Coburg and Gotha – *"that young foreign upstart"* – who represented the British Royal Household on Iona that day while his 28 year-old wife remained on *Victoria and Albert* – sketching! Perhaps the trip aboard the Royal Barge into Fingal's Cave some hours earlier had drained her, but she did give Iona a second thought: *"I must see it some other time"* she wrote in her diary. Unfortunately Victoria never returned to Iona but many of her subjects did, including her great-great-granddaughter who visited the island in August 1957, the first reigning British monarch to do so in 900 years.

Yet despite her reluctance to step ashore at Iona, Queen Victoria cut a symbolic ribbon that year.

Sir Joseph Banks, the *'discoverer'* of Staffa in 1772, Thomas Pennant, J.M.W. Turner, Felix Mendelssohn with his companion Karl Klingemann – and many others – had already sailed these seas, popularizing the area in word, image and sound, but for the foreseeable future Iona, Staffa and Oban were to receive even more attention for having been part of the *"Royal Route"*.

For those who know the area of London with its famous station, *"Charing Cross of the Western Highlands"* is a strange description of Oban as we see it today, but it was considered wholly appropriate in 1866 and with apparent good cause:

> *"Oban, the Charing Cross of the Western Highlands of Scotland, has many attractions for the tourist, afloat or ashore ... a place thriving so fast, where so many of the shops have plate-glass fronts, the villas are so handsome, the hotels so many – one of them at least, the Great-North-Western, challenging 'comparison with any house out of Oban' although Craig-Ard hotel looks down upon it – and the others, the Caledonian, King's Arms, Queen's &c., all having their own set of supporters; and so abundant is patronage at times, that it is hard to find beds..."*

The opinions of Alexander Murray as expressed in his guide **'Scotland Described'**, written for the active visitor and *"for those who may be unable to stir from home."*

Carte de Visite of Oban c.1863 by George Washington Wilson.

But if Oban was a Scottish *'Charing Cross'* where was its most important feature – the railway station? Murray had the answer:
> *"The railway from Callander, by Glen-Ogle, Strathfillan, Tyndrum, Loch-Awe and Loch-Etive is in rapid progress of construction; and when completed to Oban, the aspiring burghers there dream of Oban becoming a place of call for the Cunard steamers...".*

10

Unfortunately, the progress of the line was just about as rapid in the 1860s as the high speed rail-link between central London and the Channel Tunnel is in the 1990s. Oban children born in 1866 would all be eligible for employment with the Callander & Oban Railway Company before the first train ever reached the town! So it was the steamer and the coach – with just a little help from the train out of Queen Street station to the pier at Helensburgh – that carried patient travellers on their 13 hour journey between Glasgow and Oban via Loch Awe for a few more years after 1866.

WEST HIGHLAND COACHES.
OBAN, GLASGOW, & EDINBURGH.
Via PASS OF MELFORT, ARDRISHAIG, AND HELENSBURGH.

Oban, Glasgow, and Edinburgh, via Ardrishaig, and Helensburgh.

Ardrishaig, Loch-Awe, Pass of Melfort, Oban, Inveraray, Glasgow, Edinburgh.

Through Fares fr. Oban, via Lochawe—
Ardrishaig 12/6, Helensburgh 14/
Glasgow, 14/6 Edinburgh, 20/6

Coach leaves	Train leaves	Via Melfort.		
OBAN, *via* Lochawe..6-45 am	EDINBURGH ......6-15 am		Single	Ret.
„ Melfort ...7-45 „	Glasgow (Queen St.)..7-30 „	Ardrishaig......10/		17/
Steamer leaves	Steamer leaves	Helensburgh, ..12/		18/
Ardrishaig ....2- 0 pm	Helensburgh ....8-30 „	Glasgow.........12/6		18/6
Train leaves	Coach leaves	Falkirk 16/2		24/
Helensburgh...........6-30 „	Ardrishaig ....1- 0 pm	Polmont.........16/8		24/9
Glasgow ....arr 7-45 „	OBAN, *via* Melfort....7- 0 „	Linlithgow,.....17/6		26/
EDINBURGH....arr 9-30 „	„ Lochawe..8-30 „	Edinburgh 18/6		28/6

Drivers' Fees extra.

Having survived the trip from Glasgow, visitors could rely on the services offered by Mr George Buchanan of Messrs. Buchanan & Dick in George Street, a veritable Victorian Tourist Information office in the centre of Oban. Guide-book writers urged their readers to call in *"for all needful information as to routes for further travel &c..."* and a contemporary advertisement reveals the extent of their business, booking seats on coaches, trains and steamers on the route between Oban, Glasgow or Edinburgh; supplying local time-tables, with a map, for 1d; forwarding *Game Boxes* on behalf of their customers and even arranging vehicle hire in the shape of carriages, waggonettes and dog-carts.

Hotel accommodation, however, was not a service that Buchanan would have needed to offer. Most visitors had pre-booked their rooms, for Victorian Oban was a watering-place for the *"Nobility and the Gentry"* and they knew their status in life. To miss the *season* would have been a social disaster and their hotel apartments were reserved well in advance. But the *tourist* was a different breed altogether; an after-thought – or worse, a commercial traveller! – not to be mistaken for a knight or a gentleman, and Mrs McLaurin of Craig-Ard Hotel was aware of that fact as her 1860s advertisement shows.

OBAN—CRAIG-ARD HOTEL.

THE accommodation of this new and spacious Hotel is ample, the Rooms lofty and well-aired—near the Steamboat Pier, and commanding one of the most picturesque and extensive views in Argyleshire. Mrs. M'LAURIN, in returning thanks to the Nobility, Gentry, and Tourists, for the liberal support she has for many years received at the WOODSIDE HOTEL (which she still maintains), hopes, by sparing no exertion to secure comfort, to be honoured with the amount of patronage as on former occasions.

A decade has now gone by. It is 1.10 p.m. on a cool July day in 1877 and the 9.15 from Glasgow has just pulled in to Dalmally Station to the cry: *"Dalmally! Dalmally Station! All change here for the coach to Oban."*

Regrettably, just forty-eight of the seventy-four miles of railway track have been laid between Callander and Oban, and while the scenery may look spectacular from a slow-moving coach – especially through the Passes of Brander and Awe – the last twenty-six miles of the journey to Oban from Dalmally will take a further 3 hours and 40 minutes to complete.

		P.M.	P.M.	P.M.
LONDON (Euston), ... Leave		8.50	9.0	
		A.M.	A.M.	
CARLISLE, ..., . ,,		4.18	5.55	
EDINBURGH (Waverley), . . ,,		6.15	8.30	3.55
GLASGOW (Buchanan Street), . ,,		7.0	9.15	4.5
DALMALLY, ... Arr.		11.20	1.10	8.25
				A.M.
COACH, { DALMALLY, . . . Leave		11.30	1.20	7.0
{ OBAN, ... Arr.		3.20	5.0	10.30

In 1877, Mr. James Miller of Oban published his 386 page **"Royal Tourist Handbook to the Highlands and Islands"** and the press reviews were most favourable: *"A great advance on any we have seen"*, according to a distant critic with the *Manchester Examiner*, while the reviewer of the *North British Mail* thought it *"by far the best Guide to the West Highlands yet published"*. This, then, was *the* book to have if undertaking a journey to Oban or the Isles in the late 1870s, and the McLaurins at Craig-Ard Hotel had placed an advertisement within its pages, but what had happened to the *Nobility and Gentry* that they had been trying to attract in1866?

The wines and cuisine at Craig-Ard were still of the finest quality; a hot meal was available upon arrival of the swift steamer from Glasgow; French and German were spoken at the hotel; charges were still moderate and apartments could be engaged by the week or longer. But now the advertisement was directed at *"Anglers, Tourists and Strangers..."* and one can only assume that the knights and the gentlefolk had felt it necessary to move down to the Esplanade and into the larger establishments that fronted the sea.

With five separate banks, seven churches, a good steamer route to Glasgow, a railway heading its way and a growing population, Oban made a decision that year:

> *"...to depend in the future, as it has done in the past, on the tourist traffic, which every year goes on increasing, and will increase with the different facilities that are every year being provided by the steamboat companies. With the opening of the railway through from Callander to Oban, the tourist traffic will receive a great impulse."*

And so it was to be.

It is now 1881. Prince Albert has been dead for twenty years; former Prime Minister Benjamin Disraeli passed away in April; 62 year-old Victoria is still *Regina et Imperatrix* and the line of the Callander & Oban Railway Company – which cost £670,022 to complete – finally reached Oban last year.

Desirous of an August holiday-by-the-sea, and an opportunity to explore Staffa and Iona with his family, an English gentleman has purchased a copy of MacBrayne's **'Official Guide to Summer Tours in Scotland'** at his local railway station. The 94 page guide, within a Royal blue cloth cover embossed with gold letters and embellishments, has twelve full-page illustrations, a coloured 'Balloon Map' showing the steamer routes around the west coast of Scotland, and some useful information on departure times, fares and local excursions. Priced at 1/-, this latest edition of Mr David MacBrayne's guide was essential reading for those embarking on a tour of the Western Isles.

The departure point of our English traveller is immaterial. He and his family can travel to Oban on severe 3rd Class seats for one penny a mile or journey from London, Leeds, Birmingham or Liverpool in 1st Class luxury and enjoy *"...saloon carriages and sleeping saloons, with lavatories and other conveniences attached"*, courtesy of the London & North Western Railway Company, Midland Railway and Caledonian Railway. But as the name on the fly-leaf of this genuine 1881 edition of the guide is that of a *'Geo. Helder'* we will sneak a look inside the recently-discovered – but wholly imaginary – diary of George Helder, a fictitious London physician:

> ***Friday evening:*** *Had Wills load trunks onto the carriage and convey us to Euston for 8.50 p.m. to Oban. Rebecca very excited ... this will be her first rail journey by night and Mama has her hands full! Purchased two L & N.W.R. food baskets for the journey.*

THE ALEXANDRA HOTEL OBAN.

Victorian pictorial notepaper from the Alexandra Hotel

Saturday: *Awakened by the noise at Glasgow Station... 7 o'clock – five minutes late. Mama saw to R while I stretched my aching legs ... Toward Stirling we ate from the baskets. Half a chicken, ham and beef washed down with some claret. What a Capital Breakfast! Mama elected for sherry with hers. Rebecca had my bread and cheese with salad and chicken from the other basket.*

Arrived Oban Station at 12.42 p.m. – a fine new building. Excellent time after some 16 hours ... just two minutes off the time-table. Plenty of juvenile touters here canvassing business for the various hotels, ours is to be the Alexandra. R astonished at the size of the gulls which are not like the scrawny pigeons we see in our Square! The hotel Omnibus conveyed us to our apartment where we will remain for the next seven days...

Sunday: *Attended 11.15 English service at the Episcopalian Church... sermon a little heavy. Returned to the hotel on foot as the day was fine. First Class beef at dinner tonight.*

Monday: *Heavy rain ... remained indoors. R amused herself by travelling in the elevator every time she heard the bell ring ... the attendant (a kindly man who served his Country in the Crimea) appeared to enjoy her chatter and would not hear of me scolding her for her game! I must remember to reward him when we leave.*

Tuesday: *More rain ... read Scott's 'Lord of the Isles' and was much entertained by a guest at the piano.*

'At the 'Alexandra', Oban...", an illustration from **"Messrs. Kamdene, Barnesburie & D'Alston's Tour in the North"**, *published in Scotland by John Menzies & Co. c.1886.*

Wednesday: *Rose at 6.30 in preparation for our voyage to Iona. The Omnibus conveyed us and five more to the Pier for the 8 o'clock sail of Mr MacBrayne's 'Pioneer'. R has made friends with the daughter of Canon & Mrs Hugh Williams of Bath. She is also 10 and named Mary.*

Rain falling as we approach Craignure ... took breakfast with the Williams family on departing Lochaline ... excellent fare especially the bacon. Stopped in at Salen before reaching Tobermory, capital of the Mull Isle. Many people at the pier to greet the boat ... we learn of a Spanish galleon sunk at this place. The rain has ceased but the sun is still clouded over. Assured by the crew that it will be fine by the time we reach Staffa.

Fingal's Cave in sight ... a rare moment for us all. The Queen visited this very spot the day after my birth! The children are anxious to board the red life-boat and land on the island ... Mama has doubts. We watch the first group leave and arrive safely ... Mama relents. Made the crossing with the Canon and Mary in our boat. Mrs Williams preferred to watch and wave from the deck of the steamer! A boatman led Mary and R to Fingal's Wishing Chair ... legend is that he who sits and makes three wishes will have them granted. I asked R later if she made her wishes. She did but refused to reveal her childish secrets! We were off to Staffa near 2 hours – a most interesting place. Just before 2 p.m. the Captain blew the ship's whistle and we were away to Iona. The children waved to the life-boat until it was out of sight ... I learned that the men came out in it from a neighbouring island each day that the steamer comes this way. What a life!

2.30 prompt at Iona – how I have regarded this moment. We are to meet with a Guide appointed by the Duke of Argyll who owns the island... The place was everything the books had suggested. Saw the oldest Cross in Scotland and the graves of upward of sixty Chiefs and Kings of Scotland. Walked through the Cathedral with the Canon. Agreed that it was a sad ruin of a place though imposing in its location. Returning to the steamer we purchased some coloured pebbles and shells from a flock of bare-footed island children.
Arrived back in Oban around 5.35. It was raining! This has been a most Glorious day and one for all of us to treasure.

Victorian lithograph of Iona Cathedral c.1880.

Thursday: *Breakfasted late after our exertions of yesterday ... all slept well especially R! The day being dry I took a stroll around the town while Mama and R worked on their tatting. Saw some fine yachts in the Bay ... retired to the Oban Hotel for a lunch-time libation ... the place was full of local fisher-folk. Early dinner to-night ... we are off on a new adventure tomorrow!*

Friday: *Train trip to Loch Awe Station ... arrived 8.55. Morning warm with little wind. Mama says she will fill her sketch book today! Our boat is the 'Lochawe', compact and brilliant white tho' quite small ... A delightful trip on the Loch. We called at a little place named New York on the way! R was much amused by that.*

Arrived at Ford 10.45 ... now about to board the coach then on to Ardrishaig for the sail down the Canal on 'Linnet'. Uncomfortable coach trip but our cheery companions kept us in good spirits. What Crowds on the little 'Linnet'! Some of the passengers have taken to walking alongside the boat between the lock-gates. Not me – I might fall behind! The sun beats down but Mama is still at her sketching as I write and R has made some new friends. 3 o'clock and Crinan is reached after some 2 hours on the Canal. Returned to Oban by 4.45 aboard 'Chevalier' – a fine, busy ship.

S.S. "Linnet," Crinan Canal, Ardrishaig.

RELIABLE SERIES.

An Edwardian postcard showing the 'Linnet' on the Crinan Canal.

Saturday: *Our final day in Oban. We take the afternoon train for Euston at five past 4. R announces at Breakfast that she wishes to remain behind for a further week ...! I hope Wills remembers to meet us at 8 tomorrow morning. Mama is supervising Flora in the packing ... she has been an excellent Maid and would do well in London.*

So ends George Helder's account of his family holiday in Oban. Fictitious, yes, but not entirely improbable. Middle Class, thirty-four years old, married with one child; servants, a carriage and a thriving private medical practice situated in a leafy London square, Helder's annual income would have been in the region of £1,200 per annum, a considerable sum of money in 1881 when compared with that of a senior clerk in the legal profession who would be earning between £350 and £400 a year, or a police constable on £65 a year. Unfortunately there were no references to money or the price of goods and services in the diary since Helder was a *gentleman* and did not write about such things! However, with a little help from the Victorian guide books and time-tables of the day, it is possible to calculate the total cost of the Helder family holiday to Oban.

The price of a return Tourist ticket from London Euston was £6. 12. 3d in 1881 while the London & North Western Railway food baskets cost an additional 2/6d each. For that sum the traveller received half a chicken, with ham or tongue or a portion of beef; salad, bread, cheese and butter, and either a half bottle of claret, two glasses of sherry or a pint bottle of stout.

The steamer trip to Staffa and Iona cost 12/6d (optional breakfast at 2/- per person) and the Loch Awe – Crinan Canal – Oban tour was advertised at 20/-. An apartment or suite of rooms at the Alexandra Hotel in 'High Season' cost around 5 guineas and would have included all meals, coal fires in the room, hot baths and the services of a maid for the ladies. With extras for drinks and sandwiches away from the hotel, plus gratuities for railway porters and hotel staff, 30 guineas would have covered everything – even some small souvenirs for Rebecca.

For the family album, copies of the very latest photographic images of Oban, Staffa and Iona by Mr George Washington Wilson – Photographer to Her Majesty in Scotland – could be purchased locally and came in various sizes ranging from the small Cartes-de-Visite or Stereoscopic slides on card to whole-plate photographs. These pictures took the place of *Pictorial* postcards which were not permitted in Great Britain, although they had been on sale on the Continent since 1870. Not until 1894 did the Post Office relent and allow the British holidaymaker to send such a *"foreign thing"* as a postcard *with a picture on it!*

Oban c.1858. Stereoscopic slide number 32, by George Washington Wilson.

Argue you may (and many will before 31st December 1999) but the *20th Century* was just twenty-two days old in 1901 when Queen Victoria died and the public were drawn – quietly and solemnly at first – into the new Edwardian Age! Change was inevitable, and in Oban, private motor cars and Rankin's Char-a-banc excursions would soon replace the horse omnibus and MacIntyre's Four-in-hand coach trips to Glenshellach, although in 1906 both were still available, competing for business during the bustling days of August.

MacIntyre's

WELL-APPOINTED

COACH

Leaves East Coast Railway
Booking Office, Esplanade,
Cban, daily at 10.30 a.m.,
and 3 p.m.

FOR THE INTERESTING ROUND BY

Glenshellach, returning by Gallanach and the Sound of Kerrera.

Unsurpassed Views of Sea and Mountain Scenery are obtained during this Coach Drive.   Fare for the Round, **1/6.**

MacIntyre's coach trip advertisement of 1906...

And a photograph of the actual event...!

But if Miss Rebecca Helder were to return to Oban in August 1906, what changes – apart from the Coliseum-like McCaig Tower – would she notice after twenty-five years?

Assuming that Rebecca travelled from London Euston as previously, she might have been pleasantly surprised to find that the adult train fare was still firm at £6. 12. 3d – unchanged after a quarter of a century! A fine example of the competitiveness of the private railway companies at this time. The 8.50 p.m. from Euston to Scotland still ran – but faster – arriving in oban at 11.55 a.m., forty-five minutes earlier than its 1881 counterpart. Now it was equipped with corridor carriages, refreshment and dining cars, but food baskets continued to be available at principal stations along the route although by 1906 their price had risen by 6d to 3/- each.

The Alexandra Hotel had just been redecorated and boasted of its *"New Smoking Lounge and Verandah."* Rebecca's childhood plaything of 1881 – the Elevator – was still intact and the hotel omnibus continued to run guests to and from the steamer and railway piers, but fully inclusive daily rates in 1906 were now 10/6d per person (with a reduction for two in a room) and allowing for a half-rate for a ten year-old child, a seven night stay would have been around 9 guineas in 1906 or almost double the price of 1881.

The paddle steamer 'Grenadier' in Oban Bay; photo by McIsaac & Riddle of Oban.

The old *Pioneer* had been replaced by David MacBrayne's very beautiful paddle-steamer *Grenadier* which now departed Oban at 8.20 a.m. – twenty minutes later than the *Pioneer* – calling at the same places *en route* and allowing ninety minutes at Staffa and an hour and three-quarters on Iona. The fare had risen by half-a-crown to 15/- but for an additional 5/- passengers could purchase a meal ticket to cover breakfast, dinner and a plain Afternoon Tea. Breakfast-only was still available at the 1881 price of 2/- per person (today, a bacon sandwich on MV *Isle of Mull* costs £1 but it is highly recommended!) and a glass of whisky cost just the same as a coffee and biscuit – 6d! *Those were the days!*

A tragic end for the 'Grenadier'. At Oban's North Pier, in September 1927, a fire aboard the vessel killed some of the crew including her commander, Captain McArthur. The ship was raised and eventually broken up at Ardrossan in 1928.

The trip down Loch Awe through the Crinan Canal and back to Oban had actually dropped 5/- to 15/- per head but competition from other tour operators was particularly strong in 1906, with day trips to such places as Glencoe, Mallaig, Fort William, Callander and the Trossachs. For those on a limited budget, Rankin's Char-a-banc *Blue Bell* went out to Ganavan Sands at 10.00, 11.30, 2.00 and 4.00 p.m. each day and cost 1/- return. *"The Finest Sea and Mountain Panorama in Scotland"* was how the route was advertised. A proud boast and a delightful trip in 1906 no doubt, but one can think of finer views today.

After World War I, the seemingly idyllic days of the Victorian and Edwardian era never returned. The telephone replaced the postcard as a method of regular daily communication and the wireless brought immediate news from distant corners of the country. Motor-cars became affordable and common-place; aeroplanes flew to Paris; Talking Pictures came to Oban and ... well the list is endless. The first half of the century brought so many changes and MacBayne's had to change with it.

Visitors to OBAN are assured
of an enjoyable evening's
entertainment at

The Cinema House
George Street

where all the latest Talking Pictures are shown from the best sound reproducing equipment

Continuous from 6-30 to 10-30 each evening
Matinees on wet afternoons at 2-30

The *original* Mr David MacBrayne, sole partner of the company, relinquished his management role in 1902 at the age of eighty-eight and his sons David Hope and Laurence took control. In 1906, the business was converted into a Private Limited Liability Company with Oban banker Campbell Brown as one of its co-directors; Laurence then disposed of his interests and brother David became Chairman of the new David MacBrayne Limited. But then, in 1928, the greatest change of all occurred.

That year, mainly because of insufficient funding, MacBrayne's withdrew its tender for the conveyance of the Royal Mail and the Government failed to secure additional tenders for the service. With Highland Airways and Northern & Scottish Airways still in the future, the West Highland steamer service was crucial for the movement of mail to the islands and could not be allowed to fail, so a rescue plan was drawn up by Sir Alfred Read of Coast Lines Ltd. and Lord Stamp of the London, Midland & Scottish Railway Company. Jointly, they acquired the company of David MacBrayne – ships and all – and Sir Alfred Read became Chairman and Managing Director of the new firm of David MacBrayne *(1928)* Limited.

The famous name may have been retained but Mr David Hope MacBrayne and the Head Office at 119, Hope Street, Glasgow were not. The new company moved into Clyde House in Robertson Street, Glasgow, and H.M. Government in the shape of Lt. Col. Norman MacLeod C.M.G., D.S.O., secured representation on the board of Directors. In 1935 the company dropped the *(1928)* from its title and in 1951 celebrated *"one hundred years of progress."*

Somewhat ironically, when the pioneering airlines Highland Airways and Northern & Scottish Airways merged and reappeared as Scottish Airways Limited in August 1937, Mr James W. Ratledge, a director of David MacBrayne Ltd., was appointed to the Board of this new company!

Then came the *"Swinging Sixties"* and while the Russians put Yuri Gagarin into Space the British jumped into Mini motor-cars and roared around their earthbound kingdom. In 1965 the *Observer* newspaper, in conjunction with publisher Hodder and Stoughton, produced a cheap little paperback described as a *"guide to resorts and hotels..."* Hopelessly out-of-date now, **'Time Off in Scotland'** still provides an interesting link to the Alexandra Hotel which merited the following entry:

> *"This hotel has a good, sunny and quiet position on the esplanade. Efficiently run and remarkably inexpensive for what is offered. Airy lounge, sun lounge, bar, recreation room, Lift: garage. No dogs. Open April-October. 61 rooms, all with hot and cold water, a few with bath. Bed and breakfast 36/- to 42/-. Day, 48/- to 57/-."*

Shunning public transport, many more travellers were now arriving in Oban by car and MacBrayne's were ready for them, anxious to serve the needs of this new breed of fast-moving, *war-time-baby* visitor. And from their Head Office in Robertson Street, Glasgow, the company hired a wondrous brochure-writer who tempted the holidaymaker with the following lines:

THE ISLES OF YOUTH

> *"At this phase of the evolution of society, men and women, jostling in the layers of a mindless commercial system, are seeking another dimension for their dreams and desires."*

Quite! But he – or was it a she? – had more:

"Each day advertises a quicker and smoother way of living and the next discards a multitude of prescriptions how to breathe, to sleep and to eat.

It is a frenzied search for some place out of themselves, a shore or a hillside where they may rest and recapture the music and the breath of youth."

Still reading? Then stay with it:

"And out there, on the chord of the setting sun, lies a region that is ever new – the Isles of Youth. The morning light brings them up from the sea. They break from the mists and the summer haze like the prows of great ships coming out of the infinite ocean of time ... the road that leads to them by land and sea is a promise ... the Isles of Youth belong to another state of human affairs – another plane of experience – where the burdens of obligation and compulsion are unknown and the eye is satisfied ... Come with us then on this happy exploit."

Written in the 1930s style of that island-hopping story-teller Alasdair Alpin MacGregor, all this – and a little more besides – appeared beneath a colour photograph of Iona Abbey in the 1962 edition of MacBrayne's brochure for the Western Highlands and Islands. The Isles of Youth – from Islay in the south to Lewis in the north – were about to be well and truly *exploited!*

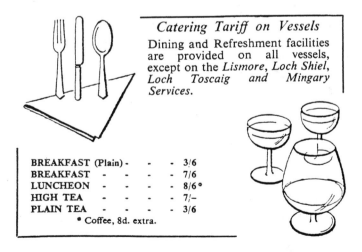

Catering Tariff on Vessels

Dining and Refreshment facilities are provided on all vessels, except on the *Lismore, Loch Shiel, Loch Toscaig* and *Mingary* Services.

BREAKFAST (Plain) -	-	- 3/6
BREAKFAST -	- -	- 7/6
LUNCHEON -	- -	- 8/6 °
HIGH TEA -	- -	- 7/-
PLAIN TEA -	- -	- 3/6

° Coffee, 8d. extra.

MacBrayne's catering charges in 1962; from their 'Isles of Youth' brochure.

Whether the islands were ready for an invasion of tourists was never really considered. Some of the passenger ships – fourteen in all at this time not including the cargo carriers and small ferry boats – were due to be replaced and generating extra revenue was absolutely essential, despite an annual Government subsidy of around £300,000. MacBrayne's were actively promoting their *"Extended Tours by Coach and Steamer"* running excursions from Glasgow to Benbecula, Eriskay and the Uists (6 days for £26. 10. 0d inclusive); to Stornoway and the Uists for 11 days at £43. 10. 0d or to Islay and Oban for an 8 day tour at £28. 10. 0d. This indeed was a positive indication as to the future and the new generation of car ferries: *Hebrides, Clansman* and *Columba*.

Even as late as 1969 – and despite the new pier at Craignure which had opened in 1963 – P.A.Macnab was compelled to write in his authoritative book **'The Isle of Mull'** (David & Charles, *The Islands Series,* 1970):

> *"Mull is not yet ready for tourism; the demand is far ahead of the organisation ..."*

The same thing was also being said of some of the Outer Isles at this time – *but that was all yesterday. A generation ago!*

The larger car ferries in Caledonian MacBrayne's current (1994) fleet are comfortable and reliable, crewed by hard-working men and women. Perhaps everything is a little too clinical and regimented now – organised and safer some will say – but many travellers still have fond memories of perilous landings at Iona from *King George V,* or of journeys made between Oban and the Outer Isles when sleeping (or smoking!) in the car while at sea bothered no one. Less fonder memories might include a nine hour voyage with an inebriate fellow-traveller in a cabin on the *Iona* – What a man! What cabins! – as she battled towards Lochboisdale in a fierce January storm; or worse, *not* reaching Castlebay from Oban and having to return directly to the mainland from South Uist after fifteen hours in yet one more winter gale. That brochure-writer – *bless him!* – never mentioned any of these things. Adventurous days they were indeed!

Today, the islands *are* ready for the tourist, prepared to receive the day-trippers, the coach parties or the long-stay visitor. Awash with coffee and bacon sandwiches we leave the ferry at Craignure, Lochboisdale, Stornoway or any port on any of the islands. We use the *"fresh air"* as an excuse for our appetites at dinner on the first night, while fruit juice, porridge, sausage, bacon, egg, black-pudding, mushrooms, toast, marmalade and a pot of tea the next morning will undoubtedly *"set us up"* for the day. But this is *your* adventure, *your* well-earned holiday, and the businesses welcome your custom, for the season is short and the winter often far too long. Prices may have been stable between 1881 and 1906 but they have certainly risen since the 1960s and bed and breakfast at the Alexandra Hotel for 42 shillings a night is definitely a thing of the past. Depending on the season and availability, a single room with breakfast will now cost £30 or more – the price of George Helder's *all-inclusive* 8 day holiday for three in 1881 – but just look at what their brochure offers today:

"... 54 en-suite bedrooms, all of which have telephone, TV (satellite also available), radio, heating and tea/coffee making facilities. Comfortable dining room with excellent views and spacious private car park within the grounds... a new leisure complex with various sporting and fun activities – featured swimming pool, sauna, steam room, solarium, snooker, indoor bowls, games room, gymnasium ... the hotel's 36 ft. motor cruiser is available for short coastal cruises."

Staffa is now in the care of the National Trust for Scotland, having been purchased by them in 1986 thanks to a generous gift from Mr John Elliott of New York – former chairman of a large advertising agency – who wished to mark his wife's sixtieth birthday. In return, Eleanor Elliott was declared *Steward of Staffa* for life. Sadly, Staffa is no longer one of the 23 Scottish islands served by Caledonian MacBrayne. The 120 mile trip from Oban to Iona via the Sound of Mull was discontinued some years ago but trips aboard smaller vessels can be made from Iona, Fionnphort, Ulva or Dervaig.

Since 1979, much of the island of Iona has also been in the care of the National Trust for Scotland although the religious and historical sites are the responsibility of the Iona Cathedral Trustees. Yet, in spite of all the changes, the people of Oban and Iona have welcomed visitors for many years and that part of your experience will *not* have altered.

In conclusion (and while it will soon be wholly obvious) it must be pointed out that this book is *not* a guide to Oban, Iona or Staffa

The compiler is a loyal supporter of the House of Lancaster with no claims to any Scottish ancestry – imagined or otherwise – and the production of a guide-book to these places would be looked upon as an unwise and presumptuous undertaking, especially by those who live there! This offering, therefore, is just a nostalgic look at the area through the medium of vintage picture postcards and photographs in the author's extensive private collection. Enjoy the cards but be warned; they were bought and posted by a very different generation of visitor between the late 1880s and the 1950s and you may find that a few things have changed with the passage of time. To emphasize the point, the ephemera and photographs of Oban on the following pages date from 1884 to 1931. Can *you* spot the differences? Some things may have gone forever – the dock-side herring-gutters for example – but Oban was, and hopefully will remain, the undisputed *Gateway to the Isles of Youth!*

GLIMPSES OF OBAN PAST

"When the tourist season once begins, Oban is bustling and gay.

Train and steamer and coach pour streams of eager pleasure-seekers into the town – all countries of the world, all ages and ranks being represented in its hotels and streets.

The shriek of the engines, the clear tones of the steamer-bells, and the rumble of wheels is heard more frequently; the hotels hoist their flags; bands play on the promenade; graceful white-sailed yachts glide into the bay and drop anchor; tourists and canvas-shoed yachtsmen throng the streets and shops; and there is a general air of bustle and of coming and going – for Oban is a place of passage and not of rest.   Tourists go to Oban simply for the purpose of getting to somewhere else..." (Extract from volume V **'Ordnance Gazetteer of Scotland: A Survey of Scottish Topography, Statistical, Biographical and Historical'.** New Edition *c.* 1894)

A view of the Alexandra Hotel in 1884.

"Happy? Of course we are!" A glass-slide taken in Dunstaffnage Castle in July 1884.

Two 1884 views on glass-slides showing the front and rear of 'Woodburn Villa' Oban, with Craig-Ard Hotel in the background. From glass-slides.

'Cawdor House' in July 1884.

Not too difficult to locate so no clues! A glass-slide also from July 1884.

During the summer months of 1889, Dr and Mrs Francis Gray Smart of Tunbridge Wells undertook a Grand Tour of Scotland and visited Oban. A gifted photographer and first President of the Tunbridge Wells Amateur Photographic Association from 1887, Dr Smart recorded the tour on over 280 glass negatives. When he died in 1913, his cameras and glass plates were gifted to a nephew. Ignored and left in a garage, they were totally destroyed during the 1940s as a result of enemy action but the Smart's personal photo album of their tour, which had long been assumed 'lost', was found in a second-hand bookshop in Cheshire in 1986 and its discovery is the subject of the book **'The Summer of '89'**. These two pictures give a flavour of Victorian Oban – when fine private yachts filled the bay and elegantly dressed ladies could stroll down the middle of George Street.

The turn-of-the century and an aged street cleaner moves along George Street with the essential tools of his pre-motor trade – a brush and shovel!

Edwardian progress, and a photographer is on hand to record the scene as a telephone pole is erected opposite the sub post-office in Albany Terrace. A clever use of the three ladders!

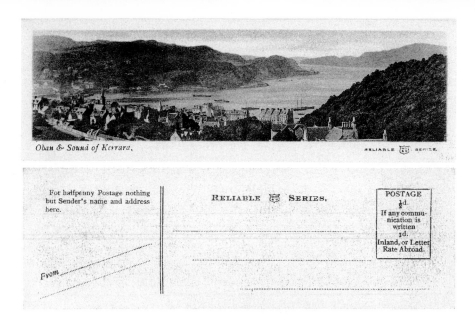

Oban & Sound of Kerrara.

RELIABLE 〔🛡️〕 SERIES.

For halfpenny Postage nothing
but Sender's name and address
here.

RELIABLE 🛡️ SERIES.

POSTAGE
½d.
If any commu-
nication is
written
1d.
Inland, or Letter
Rate Abroad.

From ....

The period from 1900 to 1914 has been called the Golden Age of the British postcard, when cards were produced in all shapes, sizes and materials include leather, wood, peat and tin! Both sides of this Edwardian postcard of Oban are reproduced almost to size.

Oban Games 1925.

Spectators at the Oban Games in 1925.

"The Railway Pier is, when the boats are discharging their catches, a busy, bustling scene, with fishermen, fishbuyers, girl gutters, porters, auctioneers, and interested onlookers all on the move..." [Alex. M. Faichney]

Photographs taken in August 1929 by H.M. Scrivens, an English photographer and artist who settled in Oban after World War I and started a successful business with premises in George Street.

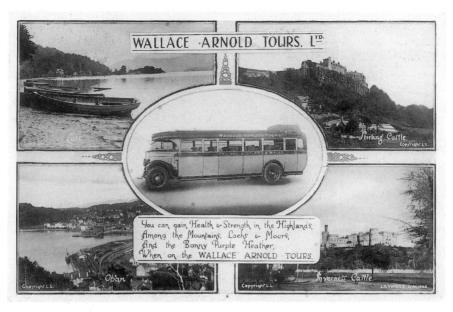

"*You must come on one of these Tours, you would enjoy it all. The hotels are all 1st Class and the scenery wonderful. How I have enjoyed it.*" *(J.A.L. Athol Palace Hotel, Pitlochry, July 1931). The writer might have been, but this author is not an employee or shareholder of Barr and Wallace Arnold Trust! This is a genuine message on a real photographic postcard produced for them by Lilywhite Ltd. of Halifax. A disastrous fire at the Lamb Mills works in 1931 destroyed tens of thousands of Lilywhite's original negatives and this picture may have been a victim. Wallace Arnold customers stay at Fishers Hotel in Pitlochry now, but one regular tour – to the Isle of Skye – includes a three night stay in Oban at the Oban Bay Hotel.*

BEHIND THE DOORS
AT 101, GEORGE STREET...

At the beginning of this century the shop situated at 101 George Street was run by Mr Samuel Lawrence, a member of the Pharmaceutical Society of Great Britain. Having removed from Glasgow some twenty years earlier, where he had received valuable experience working for Messrs. Frazer & Green – 'Chemists to Queen Victoria', Lawrence soon established himself within the town and in 1906 he advertised as being *"The Largest and Leading Chemist's Establishment in the West Highlands and patronized by Royalty..."* with a warehouse and laboratory facilities located in nearby John Street.

Lawrence's trade was regular and brisk especially during the tourist season. He opened his shop at 7.30 a.m. every day – Monday to Saturday – closing the doors at 10.00 p.m. except on Saturday when he stayed open for an extra half an hour in order to catch some of the late trade!

Sunday, however, was very different.
  "The Scottish Sabbath being fairly well observed in the Highlands," wrote the compiler of the 1906 "Oban Visitors' Guide", *"it must be understood that none of the tours enumerated in this Guide are run on Sundays."* A noble sentiment, but while MacBrayne's steamers remained tied-up at their piers and MacIntyre's coach-horses were rested, the writer of that praise-worthy sentence was able to show 'just cause' for operating his own business on the Sabbath. At 1 o'clock every Sunday, Samuel Lawrence – chemist *and* part-time publisher of *"Lawrence's* Oban Visitor's Guide"* – opened his shop for one hour then took the afternoon off. At 5.00 p.m. he reopened, closed again at 6.30 p.m. and returned at 8 o'clock for one final hour of trading. Thus were the Sabbath prescriptions of the sick and infirmed dispensed in Oban, for Lawrence stocked *"the finest drugs ... patent medicines ... infants' foods and invalid requisites."*

But behind the doors of 101 George Street there was much, much more than just Iceland Moss Cough Syrup, Beecham's Pills or Coutt's Acid for the relief of Nervousness, as the advertisements for 1906 show.

Puncture repair kits for unfortunate bicyclists or crude Lewis pottery for eager summer shoppers. A dark-room for amateur photographers who wanted to process and print their own glass-plates, or bottles of ginger beer for those cheeky housemaids from the Imperial Hotel who strolled and giggled their way up and down the Railway Pier each afternoon.

Cigarettes, cigars, pipe tobacco, or a one shilling tin of his own Asthma Remedy invention – Samuel Lawrence certainly retained a well-stocked emporium for his Edwardian customers.

39

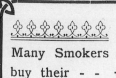

IONA – THE HOLY ISLE

"An island ... at the SW corner of the island of Mull, and separated from the long promontory known as the Ross of Mull by a channel about a mile wide, deep enough for the passage of the heaviest ships, but dangerous on account of the sunk rocks. The island lies NE and SW, and is about 3^1/2 miles long and 1^1/2 miles wide. The area is about 2000 acres, of which 600 are under occasional cultivation, the rest being pasture or waste ... there are beds of slate, quartz and marble with serpentine... It is by no means such a bleak and dismal place as it is sometimes represented to be, and there is some truth in the Gaelic proverb that asserts that if a man goes once to Iona he will go three times. The chief interest of the island lies in its historical associations with St. Columba and the introduction of Christianity into Scotland ... The village is to the E of the ruins of the nunnery, and there are a few houses in the northern district, but the southern part is uninhabited. The parish church is in the village; the stipend is £120, and there is a Manse and glebe. There is also a Free Church, the minister of which resides in Mull, and the old Free church manse is now used as a hotel..." (Extract from volume IV ***"Ordnance Gazetteer of Scotland: A Survey of Scottish Topography, Statistical, Biographical and Historical."*** New Edition c.1894)

1. Ferry boat at Pier, Fionnphort – an anonymous postcard produced *c.*1905, yet presumably still on sale in 1920 when this example was posted from Iona to the sports officer at the YMCA Camp in the grounds of Lowther College, Lytham, Lancashire: *"Am in flourishing health,"* claims the anonymous writer, *"and am helping at the hay – hope to write sometime but my notepaper is out!"* The present ferry from Fionnphort – MV *Loch Buie* – is capably of carrying up to 250 passengers.

2-3. Two cards from publisher Raphael Tuck's *"Bonnie Scotland Series"*. Reproduced from paintings by the artist Henry B. Wimbush (*d.* 1908), a six card set of Iona and Staffa views – set No. 7684 – went on sale in 1904-05. It was an immediate best-seller and individual postcards are much prized by collectors today.

4. A typical 1930s art postcard from a water-colour by Tom Gilfillan who produced posters and pictures for David MacBrayne Ltd. including a stirring *'Flags and Highland Warriors'* painting which appeared on the cover of their 1936 holiday brochure.

43

5. MacBrayne's paddle steamer *Grenadier* at the **Landing Place, Iona.** A black & white postcard – numbered 484/81 – published anonymously *c.*1906 but possibly an *"Iona Press Series"* product (see **61**). The Iona Press was a printing and publishing company founded in the 1880s with premises behind the St. Columba Hotel, in what is now the Iona Bookshop. During the brief life of the firm, picture postcards had not been manufactured for use in Great Britain and all cards marked *"Iona Press Series"* were printed after it closed down. The name, however, continued to be used by a member of the founding Muir family.

6. More **Landing at Iona** postcards – a popular and profitable subject for card producers and sellers alike over many years. This hand-coloured Stengel & Co. card of *Grenadier* was posted from Iona on 3 September 1909 and carried an urgent message to Mrs Cameron in Carrickfergus, Ireland: *"Friday morning – got here last night. Sorry, will not catch boat tonight. Will return as soon as possible, John."* The growth of the telephone system eventually reduced such *message* cards until the sending of a postcard became nothing more than a holiday ritual or a long-distance weather report.

7. The message on this card of *King George V* by J.B. White of Dundee is typical of so many. *"I sampled this method of disembarking on Monday,"* wrote A.M. to Mrs Shaw in Shipley, Yorkshire, in July 1939. *"The sea was choppy and not at all like this p.c. Iona is a desolate looking isle on a dull day & Staffa is worse..."*. Ten months later, in May 1940, *King George V* was transporting troops from Dunkirk, an arduous task recognised by the award of the D.S.O. to her Captain and Chief Engineer and a D.S.M. for the Bo'sun.

8. A picture taken on a summer day in 1890 by an employee of Valentine's of Dundee, reproduced here (and on the cover) from an original Victorian half-plate sepia photograph, the only form in which this image could be bought by the public until the British *pictorial*

45

postcard was given Post Office approval in September 1894. I am indebted to Angus Johnson of the St. Columba Hotel for bringing to my attention a letter from Dr H.F. Wilson of St. Fillans, Perthshire, to the editor of the *Oban Times* in February 1970. Then in his mid-eighties, Dr Wilson identified himself as the six-year old on the barrel, with his sister to his left and their father alongside Purser MacKay from the *Grenadier*. Incidentally, Dr Wilson's mother was the youngest daughter of African explorer David Livingstone.

Children Selling Shells, Iona   Valentines Series

9. After 1894 – with the release of the first-ever British picture postcard – many of Valentine's earlier negatives were brought out of retirement, and the second version of those **Children Selling Shells** on Iona in 1890 eventually appeared as a black and white printed postcard *c.*1898. This shell-selling business probably started in the late 18th century – who knows, maybe the monks tried it before that! – and in the 1820 edition of his "Steamboat Companion and Stranger's Guide to the Western Islands and Highlands of Scotland" James Lumsden warns that: *"On landing in Iona, strangers are beset with the natives, who offer for sale a coarse species of pebble, rounded by attrition."*

Iona from Landing Stage

10. Iona from Landing Stage – a postcard published *c.*1901 by Stengel & Co. and printed at their works in Dresden where, within two or three years of the date of this card, 250 people were employed in the annual production of 30 million postcards. Over sixty people are visible in this picture and, without exception, all the females – including the children – are wearing bonnets or wide-brimmed hats as a precaution against the sun.

A CORNER OF IONA VILLAGE

11. Photographed some thirty years after the previous picture, the thatched cottages have been replaced or re-roofed almost beyond recognition. A sepia photographic postcard by publisher J.B. White Ltd. of Dundee.

47

12. A high quality real photographic sepia postcard, produced *c.* 1898 by Oban photographers McIsaac & Riddle although they were using a negative taken ten or so years earlier. A board over the door of the single storey building on the extreme left has the words *'Post Office'* on it. Turn-of-the-century photographs show the same building with the words on the board changed to read *'Iona Post Office'*.

The Village, Iona.

484/58

13-15. Three postcard views of the Village and Street produced between 1905 and 1929. The earliest card, **The Street, Iona,** bears the imprint, *"Iona Press Series"* (see **5**) and was printed in Saxony prior to World War I. The other view of the street is a photographic card produced by Valentine's for the shipping company McCallum, Orme & Co. in 1929. The general view of the village dates from the period 1905-10 and was probably published as part of the *"Iona Press Series"*. The card has a number – 484/58 – but no other identification (see **61**).

IONA VILLAGE.

RUINS OF NUNNERY AND SOUND OF IONA

16. A real photographic 1930s postcard by Millar & Lang of Glasgow showing the **Sound of Iona** from behind the Nunnery, unusual in that two passenger vessels lie at anchor – *King George V* on the right and the 'Diesel-electric' *Lochfyne,* built in 1931. Smoke emerging from the rear funnel only betrays her identity even at this distance – her forward funnel was a dummy! During the Edwardian period, Millar & Lang claimed to be the *"Largest Publishers of View Postcards in Britain",* producing cards at the rate of 1 million a week, all of which were printed within the United Kingdom.

THE RELIGIOUS SITES

Not surprisingly, the sacred edifices of Iona feature on more Victorian and Edwardian photographs and postcards than any of the other buildings or sites on the island. Many excellent books and pamphlets tell the story of St. Columba, the history of the crosses, the Nunnery, Abbey/Cathedral and the island in general, and a short list of selected titles – old and new – is given at the back of this book.

17. When the first group of photographers visited Iona *this* was their view of the Cathedral, recorded here by George Washington Wilson in the 1860s. This reproduction is taken from an original,130 year-old half-plate photograph as sold in the book shops and gift emporia of Oban at the time.

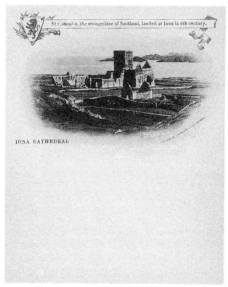

18. The earliest – possibly the very first – postcard of Iona. A *'Court-size'* card issued in 1894-5 and measuring 4.5 x 3.5 inches as opposed to the later (1899) standard size of 5.5 x 3.5 inches. Messages written on the *"Address Only"* side of postcards were forbidden by the Post office at this time, hence the large area of blank 'writing-space' on the front of this printed version of **Iona Cathedral,** published by George Washington Wilson & Co. of Aberdeen. Eventually, in 1902, postcard 'backs' were divided to allow the sender to write a message next to the address.

19. The picture on stereoscopic card No.39 – **Ruins of the Cathedral and St. Martin's Cross, Iona** – photographed by George Washington Wilson in 1860. Wilson was a great favourite with Queen Victoria and Prince Albert and responded to regular summonses to photograph Balmoral Castle and the Royal family during the 1850s. By 1856, he was advertising himself as "Photographer to the Queen" and displaying the Royal coat of arms on the reverse of his mounted photographs. *And he got away with it!* Not until 1873 did the Lord Chamberlain's office issue a warrant to Wilson at which point he could correctly claim and use the title: "Photographer to Her Majesty in Scotland."

Iona Cathedral & St. Orans Chapel.   *Island of Iona.*

Caledonia Series, No. 1440

20. Printed in Berlin but bearing the words *"Caledenia (sic) Series"*, one must assume that this was a misprint for the trade name *"Caledonia"* as used by postcard publisher J.A. McCulloch of Gorgie near Edinburgh in the early 1900s.

IONA CATHEDRAL AND ST ORAN'S CHAPEL.

21. Many of the best Victorian photographs of the Cathedral were taken from this very spot. A 1920s sepia photographic postcard in this case, published by Valentine's of Dundee who – it was jokingly alleged in 1906 – spent their time searching Scotland for the marks left by the tripod of their great rival George Washington Wilson!

Port-a-Churaich. Traditional Landing-place of St. Columba.

22. Overprinted – *"With Compliments from The Regent Boot House 330 Gairbraid Street, Maryhill"* – and carrying the wrong caption anyway, this strange black and white printed postcard was produced anonymously at some date prior to 1912. It was probably such a poor seller that, likely, the whole lot were 'remaindered off' and sold in bulk to the owner of the Regent Boot House – *cheap!*

53

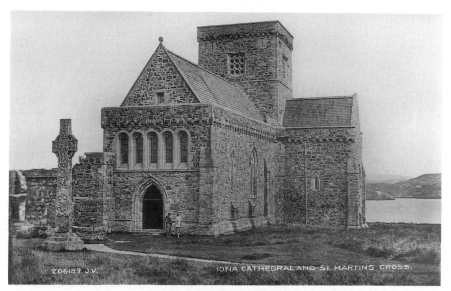

23. A 1920s sepia photographic postcard by Valentine's of Dundee, overprinted on the reverse: *"McCallum, Orme & Co. Ltd.'s Series"* and issued in July 1929, the year that the shipping companies John McCallum and Martin Orme amalgamated. The card was then sold to passengers sailing aboard the steamers *Hebrides* and *Dunara Castle* from Glasgow to the Inner and Outer Isles, including calls at Iona and St. Kilda.

24-25. Four photographic postcards produced in the 1920s by H.M. Scrivens of Oban. Such cards had a brief 'shelf-life' and were usually limited in quantity, the print-runs often being restricted to 50 or 100 cards. Scrivens arrived in Oban at the end of World War I and initially advertised himself under the address *'Maison de Photographie, Oban'*, later changed to the simpler title of *'The Studio'*.

26-27. In the period between the two Wars, the photographic output from the studios of H.M. Scrivens was prodigious. It embraced such events as funeral processions and fire disasters; a Jubilee bonfire on the island of Kerrera, Highland Games events, and a delightful postcard showing a class of Oban school-children, stood at attention in front of a gramophone, listening to a record of the King's Empire Day message!

28. The **Iona Cathedral Bell** on a postcard issued in 1931, the year the bell was cast by John Taylor & Co. of Loughborough, Leicester.

29-31. Three views showing the *interior* of the Cathedral at different stages of its reconstruction. The middle card has the briefest messages: *"I visited this, July 21, 06. H.C.C."* and was cancelled at Oban post office at 5.15 a.m. on 23 July before it went on its way to Henry M. Weeks in Skillman, New Jersey, U.S.A. Ten days later, a clerk at Skillman post office recorded its safe arrival by applying his own U.S. Receiving mark timed at 6.00 p.m. on 2 August, 1906.

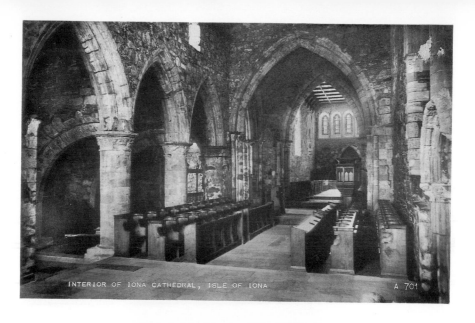

INTERIOR OF IONA CATHEDRAL, ISLE OF IONA   A 701

DOORWAY ST ORAN'S CHAPEL, IONA CATHEDRAL

32. The oldest, intact building on Iona is **St. Oran's Chapel,** the doorway being particularly beautiful and much photographed during the last 150 years. This hand-tinted postcard was issued by Valentine's of Dundee *c.* 1910.

Isle of Jona   Jona Cathedral & Tombs of the Macleans

The Wrench Series No. 8123

American Obelisk
(17. drowned)

Tombs of the MacLeans, Iona   Island 4 miles Square,
The Street of the dead   rows of graves of Lions & of Kings   Valentines Series
  Aug 18. 1903

33-34. The **Tombs of the Macleans** and the 1882 obelisk, a memorial to the dead from the American sailing ship *Guy Mannering* which sank off Iona in December 1865 while on passage to Liverpool from New York with a cargo of cotton. Two printed black & white postcards, one published by E. Wrench of London (this company ceased trading in 1906), the other by Valentine's of Dundee who finally ended their long and distinguished association with postcards in 1968.

59

Isle of Jona   *Jona Cathedral & Tombs of the Kings*

The Wrench Series No. 8122

35. Also produced by Wrench of London but printed in Saxony, this card was posted from Blair Atholl to Pitlochry in 1912 – six years after Wrench had closed down – and had probably been retained by the sender as a souvenir of a visit to the island some years earlier. Sadly, modern postcard publishers tend to reject such animated pictures. With colour reproduction being what it is, postcard-photographers concentrate more on light, shade and mood now, and highland cattle seem to make better subjects than people these days!

Isle of Iona,
Tombs of the Kings,
St. Orans Chapel
and
Iona Cathedral.

Isle of Iona. *Tombs of the Kings. St. Orans Chapel and Iona Cathedral.*

36. Bearing the logo of Stengel & Co. and marked "Printed in Saxony" on the address side, this early Edwardian postcard of the **Tombs of the King and St. Orans Chapel** is unusually devoid of human beings! With the identical picture and caption, but the number *6* at the bottom right-hand corner, the smaller illustration is reproduced exactly to scale. The reverse has all the words and details found on a full size postcard including a little box for the stamp. It could have been a trade card although there is no product mentioned. The Abbey Museum is now the resting-place for most of the stones and slabs seen in these early postcards.

The Bishop's House, Iona.

37. The Bishop's House on a sepia printed postcard with the imprint *"Iona Press Series"*. All was *not* sweetness and light when this building was proposed in the 1890s but the construction went ahead despite the arguments and petitions! The sender of the card also had her problems in August 1920: *"Did I tell you that I had lost my pretty blue dress. The new one? Stolen at Oban, I'm afraid. A very grievous loss…"*

THE VICAR OF S. COLUMB'S,
AMID THE RUINS OF IONA.
(S. Columb's Own Island).

38. An anonymous postcard of **The Vicar of St. Columb's** produced sometime before 1910, the year that this example was posted.

39. And, sadly, one more wonderful but annoyingly anonymous postcard of a **Missionary Demonstration at Iona,** the children dressed in very creative costumes, surrounding the kneeling figure of a female adult, possibly their teacher. From its general look and feel, the card is probably Edwardian.

40. The 15th century **Maclean's Cross** on the roadside by the Parish Church. A postcard produced by Stengel & Co. *c.* 1902. As mentioned elsewhere, this is not a guide-book and history has been left to those who have elected to interpret it since *'historical facts'* are often *'improved'* with the passage of time. Leaf through an *'improved...'* edition of Hugh MacDonald's **"Guide to Staffa, Iona and island of Mull"**, written some eighty years ago, and you will read that Maclean's Cross was considered at that time to be *"... of much more ancient date than any relic in the island of Iona. Indeed, testimony suggests that this cross is the oldest Christian monument in Great Britain."*!

41. Oban photographers McIsaac & Riddle managed to add a little human-interest to their late Victorian view of **Maclean's Cross.**

63

42. A different cross, a different photographer – H.M. Scrivens of Oban, a worthy successor to McIsaac & Riddle. While the crowd at this 1920s gathering concentrated their attentions elsewhere he focussed on **St. Martins Cross,** a 9th century example which, it is said, has stood on this site for 1200 years.

43. And from Valentine's of Dundee, a sepia photographic postcard issued in 1934 showing **St. John's Cross** when it was exposed to the elements. Blown-down and damaged on a number of occasions over the years, the restored Cross is now in the Abbey Museum.

MacKINNON'S CROSS.

44-45. Both sides of the elaborately decorated **MacKinnon's Cross** which dates from the 15th century and was dedicated to MacKinnon, Abbot of Iona at the time. The postcard with the white border was issued in 1909 by the publishers of Edward C. Trenholme's book **"The Story of Iona"** while the other card bears the imprint *"Iona Press Series"*.

McKinnon's Cross.

65

Ruins of Nunnery, Iona Cathedral

46-47. Even if the weather is inclement, the great majority of present-day visitors still manage to walk the short distance from ferry to **The Nunnery,** but on a balmy summer day it can be seen at its very best. These two Edwardian postcards serve as a reminder of the time before the garden was laid out, when carved stones still littered the ground with no thought given to their security or conservation. Most are now housed in the Nunnery Museum, formerly St. Ronan's parish church.

Ruins of the Nunnery.   Isle of Iona.

The War Memorial, Iona.

484/85

48. Iona's **War Memorial** to the dead of the Great War. A 1920s postcard – numbered 484/85 and probably an *"Iona Press Series"* example – sent, ironically, during the middle years of World War II.

Martyrs Bay, Iona

49. An Edwardian postcard by Valentine's of Dundee showing **Martyrs' Bay** and the U.F. Church. But a word of advice! For religious services please try elsewhere. This is now a private house.

U. F. Church, Iona.

50. A close-up view of the *former* **United Free Church** as seen on the previous postcard. This building also has a secular history, having been the site of Isabel (I.F.) Grant's first museum of Highland artifacts between 1935 and 1939. Having run out of space on Iona, Miss Grant moved, first to Laggan and then, on 1 June 1944, she opened the doors of *Am Fasgadh*, the site of the quite superb and much-visited Highland Folk Museum in Kingussie. This hand-coloured Edwardian postcard – with the number 484/90 – was probably an *"Iona Press"* product (see **61**).

51. Written in French and posted to Sarthe, France, from Inverness at 6.30 p.m. on Tuesday 30 July 1901, this early postcard with vignettes of Iona and Staffa – published by Valentine's of Dundee – was received in Sarthe on Thursday 1 August, just two days later!

68

SPOUTING CAVE –IONA   Elma Story

52-54. Watercolours of Iona reproduced on postcard during the late 1930s. The view of the **Spouting Cave** by Elma Story was published anonymously. Valentine's, however, published the **Machair** and **Sunset** cards and added the credit *"From an original water colour by E.W.H."* which wasn't much help! The pictures were actually painted by a Mr Ernest William Haslehurst but it was many years later before that gem of information came to hand.

ON THE MACHAIR, IONA

55-57. Three views of island homes prior to 1909, with a postcard by Valentine's of a croft at *Sligineach* and two further offerings from Trenholme's book (see **44**). The same **Cottages by St. Ronan's Bay** appear on cards **3** and **10**.

CNOC-CULPHAIL CROFT

COTTAGES BY ST. RONAN'S BAY

58. A type of postcard much favoured by Edwardian tourists, most of whom came from large towns, were affluent, had homes lit by gas or electric and owned a telephone. The caption: **"Natives of..."** may seem derogatory but it was simply four letters shorter than *Inhabitants,* an important consideration for a caption-writer! That said, Hebridean dwellings, dress and way-of-life were very alien, even to people from Oban, and the opportunity to visit an island – St. Kilda especially, where dozens of different cards carried the "Natives of..." caption prior to 1930 – was not to be missed. Postcard by Valentine's of Dundee *c.* 1906.

59. The **Culdee Circle,** probable site of hermit dwellings dating from the 9th century, as seen on an Edwardian postcard produced by McIsaac & Riddle of Oban, and posted to sunny Morecambe from wet Iona – *"an awful day here today"* – on 29 August 1907.

The Marble Quarries, Iona

60. Few tourists ever see the site of the **Marble Quarry** because of its location at the southern end of the island, well away from the attractions and *dis*tractions by the pier. Like the marble quarry on Skye, it, too, flourished in Edwardian times but production was brought to an end during the Great War and never resumed. Where, then, did the stone for my twenty-five year-old Iona souvenir, 7 inches high with a metal St. John's Cross set in a white and streaky green marble base, *actually* come from?

61. *"Dear Bunty ... your Auntie Annie is having a grand time here* (19 August 1922) *although the weather has been a bit 'off'...".* The spacious lounge and the wonderful view alone, makes the **St. Columba Hotel** a must for the long-stay visitor and a haven for the passing pilgrim requiring something more than just spiritual sustenance. This black & white postcard has the imprint *"Iona Press Series"* and the same style of numbering as some of the anonymous cards **5, 13, 48** and **50** – in this case 484/54.

73

S. S. Dunara Castle at Bunessan Pier

62. A *rogue* card of Mull for a purpose! The *Dunara Castle* at **Bunessan** – a postcard produced for J.L. Campbell of Bunessan *c*.1915. Launched in 1875, she sailed from Glasgow at 2.00 p.m. every Thursday with cargo and passengers for Colonsay, Iona, Mull, Tiree and the Outer Isles. Her last voyage was in 1948, after which she was broken up *but not forgotten.* For anyone still wishing to be *"close to"* the old boat, the St. Columba Hotel is an ideal place since some of *Dunara Castle's* timbers were used in the hotel after she was scrapped!

S.S. Grenadier at Iona

63. The Iona trip is over. The souvenirs and postcards have been purchased; the ship's whistle has been blown and – with a bare-foot island boy looking on – the tourists hurry down to the pier for the boat back to the paddle steamer *Grenadier* and their return journey to Oban. A popular photograph taken in the early 1890s and produced as a postcard by Valentine's of Dundee for many years. This example was cancelled at Iona post office on 18 June 1906.

74

· MONASTRII · SANCTI · COLVMBE · · SIGILLVM · MONACORVM · YENSIS ·

SEAL OF THE MONASTERY
OF St COLUMBA, IONA.

64. And finally ... the last postcard in this section comes with the imprint *"Iona Press Series"* and is a fitting reminder as to the prime source of Iona's attraction for so many people each year.

WONDROUS STAFFA

"A small uninhabited island of the Inner Hebrides off the W coast of Mull ... it is $3^7/8$ miles SW of the island of Ulva, 6 N by E of Iona, and the same distance from the nearest point of Mull... Staffa appears to have been very little noticed up till near the end of the 18th century, when Sir Joseph Banks, after visiting it in 1772, published a full account of its marvels in the second volume of Pennant's 'Tour in Scotland'... Since that time, and more especially since the introduction of steam navigation, Staffa has enjoyed abundant celebrity, and been visited by multitudes of admirers. On 19 August 1847 the Queen and Prince Albert were here..." (Extract from volume VI **"Ordnance Gazetteer of Scotland: A Survey of Scottish Topography, Statistical, Biographical and Historical."** *New Edition c.1894).*

65-66. Two impressions of Staffa – a painting by J.W. Carey on a postcard produced by MacBrayne's *c.* 1910-11 for their *"Royal Route Series"*, and a photographic card issued seven or eight years earlier by Oban photographers McIsaac & Riddle.

67. From the same *"Bonnie Scotland Series"* as Iona views **2** and **3**, these postcards were given the trade name *'Oilette'* because the first issues had a rough texture simulating the brush strokes of an original painting. Introduced in 1903, *Oilettes* brought fortune and fame for Raphael Tuck who produced thousands of different sets over the years. Comprehensive *Oilette* check-lists exist, and these cards can still be purchased at any of the many postcard fairs held somewhere in Britain *every* week of the year. Some even last three or four days at a time – useful if you have the money and the stamina!

S. S. „Grenadier" at Staffa

Stengel & Co., London E. C. 39 Redcross Street 16869

78

Isle of Staffa   S. S. *Gael* & *Herdsman* from above *Colonade*

The Wrench Series No. 8132

King George V at Staffa.

68-70. The paddle steamers *Gael* (361 tons) and *Grenadier* (356 tons) with the twin-screw steamer *King George V* (815 tons) – three MacBrayne ships photographed off Staffa over a fifty year period. The postcard of *Gael* is particularly rare. Her usual route prior to 1914 was the Oban-Gairloch run three times a week but apparently, for just one season only in 1902, she worked the Staffa and Iona route. Wrench of London published this card but, as noted previously, they ceased trading in 1906.

71. A sheet of MacBrayne's headed notepaper with its original envelope. The name *'David MacBrayne'* appears four times on these items but in 1906 the firm became a limited company and a rubber stamp has been used to add *"Ltd."* to these earlier examples. The reverse of the notepaper bears a photograph of RMS *Columba* and a full page advert for *"The Grandest Sea Trips in Britain..."*; with MacBrayne's of course!

72-74. 1930s art postcards by artist Tom Gilfillan (see **4**) who managed to make the "Landing on Staffa" look so easy! The original watercolour of **Fingal's Cave** – from which the postcard shown here and on the rear cover was reproduced – surfaced in an antique shop in Oban in the 1980s and now graces a certain lounge wall in Lancashire!

Landing Staffa.

The Royal Route Series   LANDING AT STAFFA   Registered

75. Ashore at last! Ninety minutes of adventure on a deserted island and the party clamber over wet rocks, the ladies disadvantaged by their ankle length skirts and parasols. A J.W. Carey painting on an early 1900s MacBrayne *"Royal Route Series"* postcard.

Isle of Staffa
The Clam Shell Cave

The Wrench Series No. 8130

76-77. Publishers Wrench of London and Valentine's of Dundee competing for some of the lucrative business in the postcard market with fine, similar views of the **Clamshell Cave.** Both cards produced *c.* 1905.

At the Clamshell Cave, Staffa

78-79. Two more views of the **Clamshell Cave,** both from Valentine's this time. The first, a hand-coloured card posted from Oban to Yorkshire in 1910, the other a sepia photographic postcard issued in 1931.

The Causeway.   Isle of Staffa

6 Juin 1906

Stengel & Co., London E. C. 3ª Redcross Street 10805

80-81. An excellent opportunity to compare two postcards of the same scene, one from a photograph taken *c.*1904, the other in the late 1940s. For its quality and ability to convey the majesty of the place, the Edwardian version published by Stengel & Co. and printed in Dresden, beats the later version by that ubiquitous publisher Valentine's of Dundee.

THE HERDSMAN, ISLE OF STAFFA   B 7153

The West Side of Staffa

82. It is always a pity that when a publisher produces a good postcard – especially for amateur geologists in this case – he fails to leave a clue as to the photographer, the date of the picture or the name of his own company. Apparently a commercial sepia postcard, the style of printing on the reverse of this anonymous card hints at a production date *c.*1910-15.

Fingal's Cave.

83. Whatever Mendelssohn's music might have done for the promotion of Staffa over the intervening years, there is evidence that the opening bars of his *Hebrides* Overture *'Fingal's Cave'* were written the day *before* he saw the island in August 1829. That takes nothing away from the man or his music, and surely everyone has heard of **Fingal's Cave,** depicted on this 1930s postcard by Tom Gilfillan again.

86

84. Felix Mendelssohn-Bartholdy (1809-1847). A German postcard published by Kleiner Verlag of Berlin *c.* 1910.

Fingal's Cave.

85-86. Two of the very earliest postcards of Staffa; a *'Court-size'* card (see **18**) issued in 1894-5 by George Washington Wilson & Co. of Aberdeen, and an 1899 postcard of standard size but with an undivided back containing the warning: *"The Address Only to be Written on this Side"*. Ignore the warning and eagle-eyed sorter would write or rubber-stamp a 1d surcharge on the card which the recipient had to pay if he or she wanted to read the message. The white space next to the picture was where the message *should* have been!

87. From early postcards to an even earlier photograph on a stereoscopic card – numbered 16 – and titled on reverse **The Mouth of the Clamshell Cave, Staffa.** A George Washington Wilson picture taken in 1860.

88. The second Henry Wimbush art card of Staffa (see **67**) from the *"Bonnie Scotland Series"* set No. 7684 by Raphael Tuck.

89. A particularly rare French advertising postcard issued by Chocolat Lombart of Paris *c.* 1906. "Les Merveilles de la Nature" sub-titled **"La Caverne de Fingal (Ecosse)"** with the worrying addition – "La Chasse aux Mouettes" – hunting seagulls! Not, however, an unusual occurrence during the first two decades of this century. Bored passengers on the *Hebrides* and *Dunara Castle* would occasionally let loose at the birds.

90. Less worrying than the previous example, the old **Dew of the Western Isles** whisky label appeared on bottles *c.* 1900 and was reproduced on a modern postcard published by Survival Kitsch of Inverkeithing in 1986 from the Scotch Myths archive. As good a reason as any for collecting inexpensive modern postcards alongside the rare, and sometimes costly, examples from the past. A collector could expect to pay between £20 and £25 for the French advertising postcard.

91. Postcards showing the view from *within* Fingal's Cave were obvious favourites. Stengel & Co. issued their card *c.* 1902 and Valentine's had the same idea, producing a similar version at about the same time.

92. This rival Edwardian postcard by Valentine's of Dundee shows six men standing at the mouth of Fingal's Cave watching a boat-load of passengers arriving from the paddle-steamer *Grenadier*. By 1936, however, the *Grenadier* was no more (see page **22**) and a new card was required.

93. Valentine's next postcard from Fingal's Cave shows *King George V* and was issued in 1936. But don't those six men look familiar? And that boat-load of tourists! That poor woman at the stern is still with us, wearily hanging on to her parasol after 34 years at sea. And she was *still* at Staffa in 1953 when an up-dated version of the postcard went on sale in Oban. The dark-room technicians in Dundee were crafty people!

94. A calm day at Staffa, time to leave the island and return to the steamer. The photographer certainly had luck on his side on *this* day. Unidentified initials – apparently C.Z. Co. – appear in the corner of this black & white printed postcard *c.* 1904.

95. A final view of the much-loved *King George V* off Staffa. A postcard issued by Valentine's in the early 1950s.

96. One trusts that this painting was a figment of the artist's imagination; the sea looks exceptionally rough and the postcard is very green – *all over!* Publishers Raphael Tuck – *"Art Publishers to their Majesties the King and Queen"* – named this their *"Emerald Rough Sea Series"* with the sub-title *"The Scotch Coast Series"*. It was printed in Austria *c.*1908.

97. A mid-Victorian lithograph of the **Scallop or Clam-Shell Cave.**

1– HERDSMAN ISLAND.

2 FINGALS CAVE

3– WEST SIDE.—
4–The Colonnade.

W.C. Keene

VIEWS IN STAFFA.

98. A cutting, taken long ago now, from some Victorian magazine, sadly not identified. The reverse side carries a very matter-of-fact report of a tour around Scotland with such comments as: *"...the scenery is pretty, but not remarkable,"* or *"the canal meets the sea at Ardrishaig."* The best however is reserved for Bute where the climate was *"...exceptionally mild, and the island is a northern Devonshire."* That must have pleased the good people of Bute!

99. A *"Clan Tartan Heraldic Series"* postcard *c.*1910 from a very extensive range, produced entirely in Great Britain by Stoddart & Co. of – *Halifax!* The first **MacDonald of Staffa** was Colin of South Uist in 1785. Alastair de Watteville, owner of Staffa in the 1970s, refers to this ancestor in his Staffa book and recalls how the MacDonalds were forced to sell the island in 1816 because of money problems. Not surprising really, for these Regency lads enjoyed their drink! The 1810 wine bill of one more Uist MacDonald who went *bust* – MacDonald of Clanranald – is in this author's collection; in 16 months he purchased £791 worth of fine Madeira, Burgundy and Champagne from one Leith supplier – a sum roughly equal to £20,000 today.

100. The last illustration should not be taken *too* seriously but every collector picks up the occasional odd item now and then. It was issued as an excuse to *'commemorate'* the Queen Mother's 80th birthday in 1980 and purports to be a First Day Cover from Staffa, but as long as they are cheap, one can still enjoy these frivolous *Cinderella* pieces. Who knows, in 2080 someone might be delighted to find this *very* cover inside a copy of this book on a shelf in a second-hand bookshop!

SELECTED READING

Argyll, Duke of	Iona (1899 edition)
Brooks, J.A.	Welcome to Iona (1987)
Duckworth, C.L.D. & Langmuir, G.E.	West Highland Steamers (various editions from 1935)
H.M.S.O.	Iona (1988)
MacArthur, E. Mairi	Iona: the living memory of a crofting community, 1750-1914 (1990)
	That Illustrious Island ... Iona through travellers' eyes (1991)
MacCulloch, Donald B.	Staffa (1975 edition: earlier editions with different titles)
McNeill, F.M.	Iona: A History of the Island (various editions from 1920)
Ritchie, A. & E.	Iona Past and Present (various editions from 1928)
The Iona Community (Tom Graham)	Iona Abbey – a short tour (n.d. 1980s)
Trenholme, E.C.	The Story of Iona (1909)
Watteville, Alastair de	Staffa: Home of the world-renowned Fingal's Cave (1993)

This brief list contains just one book *without* the word 'Iona' or 'Staffa' in the title; **"West Highland Steamers"** by Graham Langmuir and C.L. Duckworth, who died in 1953. Originally published in 1935, this title has been revised and reissued over the years and continues to give immense pleasure (while conveying valuable facts) to many devotees. Most of the references to MacBrayne's ships in *this* book are drawn from "West Highland Steamers" with an acknowledgement now recorded here. No one has ever asked, but alongside the obligatory copy of The Bible and The Complete Works of Shakespeare, this book is *my* choice for that desert island! Mr and Mrs Langmuir have spent many a happy hour on Iona together and I trust that they will continue to enjoy the hospitality of the island.